Chickens from Scratch

RAISING YOUR OWN CHICKENS FROM HATCH TO EGG LAYING AND BEYOND

Janet Garman

JANET GARMAN

authorHOUSE®

AuthorHouse™
1663 Liberty Drive
Bloomington, IN 47403
www.authorhouse.com
Phone: 1 (800) 839-8640

© 2015 Janet Garman. All rights reserved.

No part of this book may be reproduced, stored in a retrieval system, or transmitted by any means without the written permission of the author.

Published by AuthorHouse 01/23/2015

ISBN: 978-1-4969-6484-7 (sc)
ISBN: 978-1-4969-6485-4 (e)

Any people depicted in stock imagery provided by Thinkstock are models, and such images are being used for illustrative purposes only.
Certain stock imagery © Thinkstock.

This book is printed on acid-free paper.

Because of the dynamic nature of the Internet, any web addresses or links contained in this book may have changed since publication and may no longer be valid. The views expressed in this work are solely those of the author and do not necessarily reflect the views of the publisher, and the publisher hereby disclaims any responsibility for them.

Contents

Chickens From Scratch 1

Bringing Home Chicks 4

How Many Chicks Should You Start With? 8

What Breeds of Chickens do You Want? 9

What to expect when you bring the chicks home 11

Poopy Butts. (Pasty Butt, Sticky Butt) 13

Chick Growth and Development. 16

More on Feather Development 17

Egg Laying 18

Egg Color 20

Broodiness and Aggressive Nesting Chickens 23

Introducing your chicks to an existing flock 25

Water, Food and Shelter 26

Treats and Snacks 33

Housing and Shelter 36

Chicken Behavior and Management 44

What to do if you get a Rooster? 48

Sick Chickens 50

A Few Cautions 51

Worming 52

Flying out of the Coop 53

Bumble Foot 55

Predators 57

First Aid Supplies 60

Chicken Care Notes 67

This book is dedicated to my husband Gary. I always knew I would feel at home and at peace while farming. Thank you for sharing that dream and making it become a reality. I love you more than I love the chickens.

Chickens From Scratch is my own work and contains information based on our years of experience in farming and raising chickens and other animals. It is not meant to be an all-inclusive guide to raising chickens, or a veterinary reference. Whenever in doubt, seek the advice of a licensed veterinarian in caring for your animals.

Photo Credit

I need to profusely thank Leigh Schilling Edwards for assisting me with many of the photos in this book. Leigh's work can be found in many publications and on her website, **http://naturalchickenkeeping.com**

Art Credit

The hand drawn art was prepared by Jacqui Papi. Thank you Jacqui. It was the perfect addition to my book. Your talent is second only to your kindness and giving nature.

Chickens From Scratch

Raising your own chickens from hatch to egg laying and beyond

                                        --- **by Janet Garman**

You have decided to add chicken keeping to your daily adventures. Congratulations! It has been one of the most enjoyable aspects of our homestead years. Those sweet little balls of downy softness grow and provide endless entertainment until one day, you find a freshly laid egg in the coop and your life is changed forever for the better. Nothing can compare to the daily egg gathering on the farm. The knowledge that these sweet birds create a viable food source for your family is very rewarding. Where do you get these little fluff balls? How many should you start with and what do you need to get started with poultry are just some of the many questions you will have. This book will give you the straight forward answers on the materials, knowledge and mindset you need in order to be successful with raising your own chickens. There are many and varied opinions about chicken raising. These are the practices that have worked well for us. I have also included tips and strategies that I have learned along the way from trusted sources and friends that also raise chickens, even if I did not have an opportunity to put it in practice here.

We raise egg laying breeds. Meat birds are similar in many instances but the end result comes earlier and is final. One day I hope to raise some meat birds. But, this book will be focused on chickens that are kept for the egg laying purpose.

CHICKENS FROM SCRATCH

Read through a few resource guides on chickens before taking the plunge. It will help you make a decision when looking at all those cute little cheeping chicks. Know what a healthy chick should be acting like.

Ask questions. Store personnel should be willing to answer your questions about chicken care. Likewise, a hatchery should be willing to advise you over the telephone. Knowing the basics of chick care will make you feel more at ease and ready to take over the care of the new chicks.

Bringing Home Chicks

Before bringing home the chicks, prepare the place that you will bring them home to. Make sure you have a sturdy box or bin to house the chickens. A large plastic tote is a good example of a type of box that can be used as a brooder.

Where do you purchase chicks? Purchase your chicks from these sources or see if a neighbor is letting a broody hen hatch out some eggs. Maybe you have a farmer at the local farmers market that raises chicks.

CHICKENS FROM SCRATCH

Local feed store

Mega farm supply chain retailers

Mail order hatcheries

Specialty breeders

Poultry swaps

Since the chicks need continual heat, purchase a new heat lamp and bulb or make sure that your existing heat lamp is in working order. Have the food and warm drinking water ready for the chicks.

This is how I set up my brooder box.

1. Find a safe steady surface for the box to sit upon. Consider possible reactions of any household pets when choosing a location for the brooder. If you have a pet that is curious or aggressive, make sure that the room can be secured when you are not supervising. Remember, the dog or cat is only reacting by instinct, as nature intended.
2. Fill the brooder with about 1 inch of pine shavings (cedar shavings are not recommended due to respiratory concerns). There is no need to fill the brooder too full with shavings, because you will want to change the shavings regularly to keep the brooder clean. There is no need to waste the shavings.
3. Place a thin brick or paving stone into the box. Place the waterer and feeder on the stone. This will help keep both a little cleaner when the chicks kick the shavings around. Always use warm water for the baby chicks.

4. Hook up the brooder lamp, positioned over the brooder and safely anchored by the attached clamp. Start at approximately 5 inches off the top of the box, directing the light into the box. Each week the light can be raised slightly to gradually lower the temperature in the box.

5. When using a plastic tote as a brooder, you can modify the lid and add a screen, or simply go without a lid, until the chicks begin jumping and flying a bit. To make a lid, cut a hole out of the lid using an Exacto knife, leaving a plastic frame. Using a piece of chicken wire, screen or hardware cloth, attach the wire to the frame with small bolts and washers. Or, you could just weigh the wire down with books or something heavy enough to hold it in place.

Bedding – Straw is not the preferred bedding for hatchlings. Since their legs are still weak. Walking on slippery straw can lead to a condition called spraddle leg. The same is true for newsprint. Instead, we recommend using pine shavings or paper towel to line the brooder box. After the first few weeks, and when the chicks have grown and developed a little bit more, it is fine to switch to straw or newspaper.

Some people like to use sand as a base for the brooder. Personally, I would not recommend it for small chicks because they may confuse it with the crumbled feed. While a small ingested amount would probably not hurt them, I tend to err on the side of caution.

Keep the chicks area near 100* F, the first week. Reduce the heat by 5 degrees each week until the outside temperature is above 65 * F at night and the chicks have grown feathers.

> **Brooder Temperature**
>
> You do not need to have a brooder thermometer. Check the temperature by looking at the chicks' behavior. Chicks that are too cold will huddle together under the light. Chicks that are too warm will try to stay out from under the light and be at the outer regions of the brooder box.

How Many Chicks Should You Start With?

The number of chicks to start with will be somewhat dependant on some factors, such as how many eggs do you use each week, how many chickens are you able to keep in your neighborhood, and how many can you care for. Some areas have rules about the number of chickens that are permitted in a residential yard. Also, consider that as your chickens get older, they will produce fewer eggs after the second year, and you will still need to care for them, or have another plan in mind, such as the stew pot or use as a broody hen.

If this is your first time raising and caring for chicks, I recommend starting with 3 to 6 hatchlings. Also, when ordering from the hatchery, it is a good idea to order sexed pullets. This cannot be 100% guaranteed that all the chicks will be hens but the odds are better. You may still have a cockerel in the bunch but you can cross that bridge later.

What Breeds of Chickens do You Want?

There are so many choices, it can be confusing. The following are my favorites for new chicken owners but this is just my opinion, based on selling chicks and raising my own. I chose these breeds for their temperaments, hardiness, egg laying rate, availability, and colorful feathers.

This list is by no means all inclusive.

Buff Orpington
Silver or Gold Wyandottes
Rhode Island Red
Barred Rock
White Leghorn
White Rock
Speckled Sussex
Brahmas
Gold Star
Black or Red Sex Links
Ameraucanas/Auracanas Sometimes referred to as Easter Egg breeds because they lay green or blue eggs. The eggs can also be white, brown and pinkish.
New Hampshires

Silkies have sweet temperaments and many people love having them. You will find if you ask 10 people to name their favorite breed of chicken, you will get at least 8 different answers!

Photo credit Leigh Schilling Edwards

What to expect when you bring the chicks home

The chicks are babies and if you get them soon after their arrival at the store, they will be sleepy off and on. The naps should be mixed in with periods of activity and eating and drinking. Don't be too concerned when they peck at each other unless you should see bloody spots or that one chick is having difficulty getting up and is being pecked at by the others. A natural pecking order will be established even in small chicks.

Photo credit Leigh Schilling Edwards

Pecking order is a normal behavior for the chicks. They will begin sorting this out at just a few days of age. Watch for signs that it is getting out of control and if pecking causes wounds or blood to appear. Cover any blood or red spots with a product called BluKote, which can be found in most farm supply stores. A quick spritz of Blu-Kote will turn the red area blue and stop the pecking. Watching pecking order develop can be hard for soft hearted people. Letting the chicks work it out really is the best response, while being alert for injuries.

Make sure the chicks have plenty of room to roam around. The chicks will outgrow the brooder box in a few weeks and need to transition to a grow out area, that is kept warm and safe, until they are grown and fully feathered. Some options for a grow out pen include a large dog crate, a brooder pen, or a toddler wading pool.

In most cases, one day you will return home to find your adventurous chicks have found a way out of the grow out pen and are loose in your home! At this point, or hopefully before, I add a piece of chicken wire over the brooder/grow out pen to contain the fledglings.

Poopy Butts. (Pasty Butt, Sticky Butt)

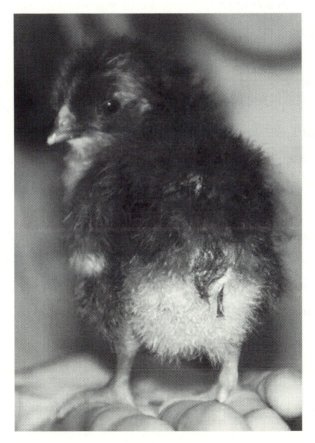

Photo credit Leigh Schilling Edwards

Around two or three days of age until approximately two weeks of age, a chick may develop a clog at the vent. Look for this in your chicks and follow this method to remove the clog. . Do so carefully so as to not tear the skin around the vent. Failing to remove the clog will most likely result in death

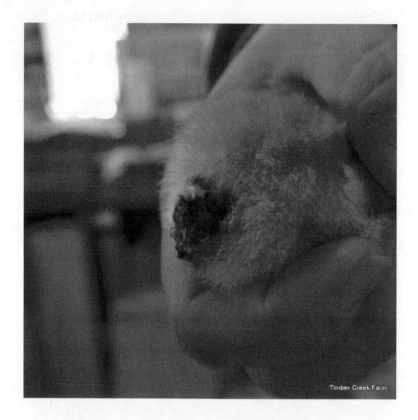

1. Put warm water in a small shallow dish
2. Carefully dip the backend of the chicken into the warm water and hold there for a few seconds.
3. Wet a paper towel with the warm water and gently dab at the poop clog until it begins to let loose from the surrounding skin and downy feathers. DO NOT PULL AT THE CLOG. You can seriously hurt the chick by being impatient and pulling the clog off.

4. Dry off the chick and put it back with the flock of babies. Continue to watch for a recurrence. As the chicks grow, this becomes less of a problem, since most pasty butt issues are gone by two weeks of age.

Chick Growth and Development.

As your chicks grow you will start to see real feathers begin to develop. You should be seeing feather development by three weeks of age and most chicks will be fully feathered enough by 10 weeks to move to an outside coop depending on the weather. Prior to moving your chicks to an outside shelter, you can and should, expose them gradually to the outdoors and dirt, grass, and insects by taking them out on warm sunny days for a time. Let them experience their first outdoor dust bath! They will enjoy hunting for bugs and spreading their wings. Make sure you put them into a wire enclosure that they can't escape from or you will lose some! Those little chicks are fast movers!

Photo Credit Leigh Schilling Edwards

More on Feather Development

As the chicks transition from down to real feathers, you will see them go through a very scraggly period of time where they look unkempt and ruffled. We refer to this as the teenage years. This is normal and they will soon out grow it. By the time your new hens are ready to lay eggs they will be fully feathered out, glossy and beautiful.

Photo Credit Leigh Schilling Edwards

Egg Laying

One of the most often asked questions is, "When will my chicken start giving me eggs?". After all, that's probably why you bought them in the first place. Most hens will begin laying around 20 weeks of age. If you buy a few chicks in the spring, you can look forward to fresh eggs by late summer or fall. Of course, there are those that just have to be at either end of the egg laying spectrum. Some may take almost 26 weeks to lay that first egg. It takes a hen approximately 25 hours to develop an egg to lay. If you are raising chickens to supply your family with fresh eggs, you may have purchased certain breeds because of the color of egg that they lay.

The color is the last thing applied to the egg as it leaves the "egg factory", except in the green and blue egg layers. The color is more built into the egg shell in those breeds.

The first eggs from many breeds of chickens will be slightly small. Don't be concerned. These are referred to as pullet eggs. The egg size should gradually increase over time. Most hens will reach their egg laying prime towards the end of their first year.

Egg Color

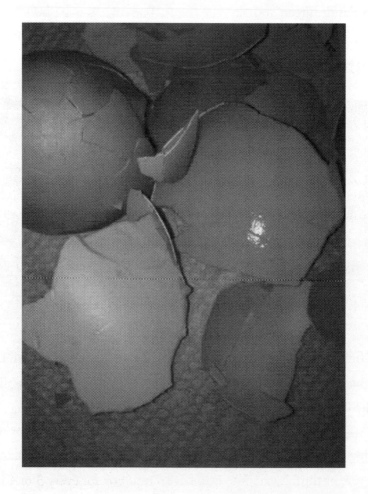

Most of the hens we own are brown egg laying breeds. These include Barred Rock, Wyandottes, Black and Red Sex Links, Rhode Island Reds, New Hampshires, Jersey Giants, Orpingtons and Astralorps.

White Leghorns lay a large white egg.

Araucanas and Ameraucanas lay the greenish and bluish colored eggs and can also lay different shades of browns and pinks. It is possible to gather enough variety of these breeds to almost have an Easter egg assortment of egg colors. This is why the breed is sometime referred to as an Easter Egger.

Nesting Boxes

Most experienced chicken owners will tell you that no matter how many nesting boxes are available, the hens will all want the most popular box! The rule of thumb, though, is to have a nest box for every 3 or 4 hens.

Nesting Boxes can be wooden crates, small animal crates, plastic tubs, commercial nesting boxes, or even a secluded area of the coop.

We have settled on using the wooden crates that can be found at flea markets and yard sales. Mostly, I just like the rustic look of them, and lined with bedding and straw, they make a nice nesting box. My neighbor, uses plastic storage bins lined with pine shavings and placed under a shelf with enough clearance over top.

I have seen very nice set ups with nesting boxes attached to the coop wall and curtains added for privacy. And I have found eggs in unique hiding places inside my coop and nowhere near a nest box.

> **One note of caution. Make sure the box is secure in its position. We lost a favorite chicken during a hot spell once. The hen must have been standing on the box and it flipped over, trapping her under the plastic bin.**

Broodiness and Aggressive Nesting Chickens

It can be disconcerting to find that one of the hens has decided to sit in the nest box and cover the eggs. Not to worry, she is just broody, hoping to hatch out a clutch of chicks. This behavior may not be OK with you, and so you will need a strategy to break her of the broody behavior.

First, if you do not have a rooster, the eggs will not be fertilized, and will not develop into chicks. Allowing a hen to sit on unfertilized eggs, is pointless, and can weaken the hen's health. When hens are brooding, they eat less, usually only getting off the nest once or twice a day to relieve themselves, get a drink and eat.

Second, if you are keeping hens for eggs for your family, you will want those eggs she is sitting on! My hens are used to me reaching under them. I rarely leave eggs in the nest boxes for long. This does not mean that my hens are always agreeable to me taking the eggs they are sitting on. I wear gloves and this affords me the courage I need to reach confidently under the screaming, biting, pecking momma wannabe and grab the eggs. I just do it. I don't apologize. Those eggs are mine! Seriously, though, you are raising chickens for eggs, so allowing the broody hen to control the situation is not in your best interest. Now, I have seen some hens that are serious about wanting to be broody. They will sit in the nest even after the eggs are gone. I toss them out in the run, only to find that they are back in the nest in a few minutes. Sometimes a short dip in cool, NOT COLD, water will break the broodiness. Sometimes, I have had to close off the coop during the day to prevent access to the nest. Of course, this means no one else can get in to lay eggs either. Another, tactic is to put the broody hen in a large dog crate with food and water for a day or so to try to break the broodiness. It just takes time and consistency.

Introducing your chicks to an existing flock

Gradually introduce the chicks to the current flock using a dog crate, or other wire type enclosure. The older chickens can see the new babies but will not be able to attack them. Over a few days time, the chicks will not be so interesting. Supervise any time they are together until this behavior calms down. When you finally put them together, do it in the evening when closing the chickens in at night. Most chickens will go to roost and not be worried about the newcomers. In the morning, hopefully, it will be business as usual. If the chicks peck each other and draw blood, use a product called BluKote to cover the red area. Leaving a reddened sore will lead to further pecking.

Water, Food and Shelter

These are the three main things you will be providing for your flock. Access to **water** is needed at all times. For the chicks, use a waterer or water fount to help prevent drowning. An average full grown chicken will drink one to two cups of water per day. Of course, water intake is dependant on the weather, but regardless of the weather being hot or cold, make sure the chickens have water. Check the water frequently to be sure it has not frozen or become too hot. Placing water founts in the shade in the summer and the sun in the winter will help. Keep water founts or containers clean.

Food

Photo Credit Leigh Schilling Edwards

For the first 20 weeks of life, the chicks should be fed a starter ration, from a reputable feed company such as MannaPro, Purina Mills, Southern States, Nutrena, or Countryside Organics. This feed is especially formulated for the growth needs of the chick up until laying age. Feeding exclusively corn deprives the chick of many nutrients and vitamins while developing. You will raise a more robust, healthy hen by giving the chick a good nutritional start. Another concern is Calcium and the calcium/phosphorus balance in the feed. Chicks fed an adult layer feed will ingest way more calcium than needed and will grow bones too quickly, leading to weak bones.

Chicks from hatch to 20 weeks need a higher level of protein, and a lower level of calcium than their older sisters. For this reason, I recommend using a chick starter ration that is perfectly blended to have the right protein level and the right balance of calcium and phosphorus. Feed chicks free choice, and keep the feeder clean of any droppings. Chicks that don't get enough to eat are slow to grow and may end up being weak layers later. Having the food available all the time, gives the chicks that are lower on the pecking order time to get plenty of food too.

It is acceptable to offer your chicks some treats after the first couple of weeks of life. I recommend waiting to ensure that the chicks are eating enough of the complete diet in the chick starter first. Some things to try are very finely chopped up pesticide free grass, scrambled eggs, small bits of finely chopped vegetables. Remember that these should be considered treats and fed in small quantities so as not to disrupt the intake of complete chick starter diet.

Feeding a Mixed Age Flock

If you have chickens of various ages, and have some layers and some chicks that still require a starter ration, it is better to feed a starter ration to all the flock and add calcium free choice for the layers to eat. Surprisingly, the chicks will not eat the extra calcium that they do not need.

Chickens are omnivores. They can eat almost anything. Bugs, greens, fruit, vegetables, worms, frogs, rodents and lizards are all on the chicken's menu. Chickens are not vegetarians. In order to get the best egg production from your chickens, we recommend a balance of using a layer ration, and supplementing your flock's diet with fresh food scraps and letting them dig for bugs, grubs and worms in the grass. Scratch grains are meant to be considered a treat. We joke that Scratch is like the candy of the chicken world. Give as a treat, to ensure the chicks will stay warm during cold spells. Do not overdo the scratch during hot weather as it can produce too much extra heat while being digested.

Timber Creek Farm

Daylight Hours and Egg Production

Length of daylight can affect egg laying, especially in colder, northern climates. We live in a fairly temperate mid Atlantic region so our winters are commonly mild and our days are sunny. Our chickens have no problem laying eggs year round and we always have plenty to share with our neighbors. But, in colder states and regions of the country and globe, chickens may almost cease egg production during the winter months. To encourage them to lay more eggs some will choose to add artificial light to the coop during winter. The extension of daylight will likely stimulate an increase in egg production. Caution! The seasons and the extra darkness are nature's way of letting the chicken's reproductive tract rest and allow the chicken to stay warm by using the feed to add fat. Interfering too much with nature can cause a chicken to be stressed and become sick. Limit the amount of additional light provided to an extra hour or two maximum. If you need to use a heat lamp, using a red bulb will not interfere with the chicken's egg production cycle, as a white light will.

Molt

Adding protein during molting.

Molting is what happens once or twice a year to a chicken as it loses its older feathers and begins to grow new feathers. During this time, many chickens will lay fewer eggs or stop laying eggs all together. The hen is redirecting the protein into feather growth instead of egg production. During molting, it may be beneficial to supplement the protein in the hen's diet with some additional protein rich treats. Meal worms, dry cat food, canned tunafish, and cheese can be given occasionally to boost the protein level in the diet. Be careful not to overdo these foods or you may wind up with a chicken with digestive upset too.

Photo Credit Leigh Schilling Edwards

Treats and Snacks

One of the fun things about owning chickens is bringing them kitchen treats. There are, however, some foods that are potentially toxic to chickens and should not be given to your flock.

DO NOT GIVE

Raw potatoes
Onions
Avocado/guacamole (the covering to the avocado pit is toxic)
Fried foods (while not toxic, they can lead to digestive upset)

GOOD FOODS TO USE AS TREATS

Vegetable scraps

Salad scraps

Cut up grass or grass clippings (as long as your yard is not treated with herbicides or pesticides)

Some weeds Chickweed, in particular is very healthy for chickens.

Cooked eggs

Limited milk products (due to high concentration of calories in dairy products)

Cooked pasta and rice

Raw pumpkins and seeds and other squash

Watermelon

Oatmeal

Flax seed

Supplements

Grit- needed to help grind up whole grains and scratch

Calcium - needed to supplement especially if the egg shells are weak or bird is laying soft shell eggs

Natural supplements include fresh herbs, apple cider vinegar and garlic

Housing and Shelter

Housing is a very important factor in raising chickens. Today, free range is a popular thought, in the chicken raising world. However, true free range chickens can annoy your neighbors and you can and will lose birds to predators.

Other Coop Options

Chicken Tractor

Cages

A section of a garage

Outdoor shed (coop) with an attached fenced in yard

A pre-made chicken coop structure

The shelter must be large enough for the number of birds you are raising. The standard recommendation is to have 3 to 4 cubic feet of space per bird. Include areas for nest boxes, and roosting space. Chickens will roost on a ladder propped against the coop wall or a 2 x 4 attached to the walls.

Design your chicken coop so that it will be easy to clean. In larger coops, having a people sized door in addition to any small drop down doors for the birds will make cleaning the coop so much easier. In smaller coops, make sure there is roof opening access for reaching injured or sick chickens and for collecting eggs.

Adequate ventilation is a must. Do not make the coop air tight. Chickens will stay warm just by being out of the weather and wind and do not need an insulated or air tight home. A draft free space with adequate ventilation will allow any ammonia odor to escape the coop and keep the flock breathing easier.

CHICKENS FROM SCRATCH

We converted an old 10 x 18 garden shed into a chicken coop. Nesting boxes are along the long wall. Roost bars are nailed into the building side walls. Windows were cut into the siding and doors for ventilation. The windows are covered with hardware cloth to keep predators out. In the winter months we cover the openings with pieces of Plexiglas to cut down on any wind or rain getting into the coop.

If you use a large shed, you may want to hang a box fan during the summer months to keep the air circulating. This should combat the extreme heat well enough to keep the coop livable. Of course this will require that your coop have some sort of electricity available. If you can have electricity available, you can also use a heat lamp in the coop if necessary or add a light to the coop in case you need to check on the chickens after dark. Caution is advised when using lights of any sort in the coop. We normally do not leave the light on when unattended due to the fire hazard this would present. That being said, I must also state that we live in a fairly moderate climate. Our chickens do not need heat during most winter weather. Having them in a secure coop gives our chickens enough protection from the elements. If you live with severe winter weather, you will have to decide on using more insulation or adding a source of heat to the coop. Chickens are actually quite cold hardy and you will lose more chickens from extreme heat than from extreme cold as long as they have some protection from the elements.

Any type of housing that will keep your chickens safe is preferable to free ranging. The biggest predator threats in our area are raccoons, opossums, rats, owls, hawks, roaming dogs, and foxes. Of course, if you are living in an area that has larger predator animals, such as coyote, bobcats, mountain lions, etc. you will need to learn the habits of those predators and take precautions accordingly.

Burying about 8 to 10 inch strips of chicken wire around the perimeter of the coop yard will prevent predators from digging into the coop area. You can also prepare the ground immediately around the coop this way. Dig a trench around the coop or pen. Bury the wire in the trench and back fill the dirt over it.

Added Heat and Cooling

Photo Credit Leigh Schilling Edwards

In my experience, living in the mid-Atlantic region, we are more apt to lose a chicken to heat stroke than to extreme cold. But, the truth is, chickens are more tolerant of cold temperatures than heat in any climate. If you live in an extremely cold area of the world, you will need to make adjustments to the coop for winter weather. Be aware that chickens do not need the coop to be as warm as our houses usually are. They will be fine, if insulated from a cold draft, kept dry and kept healthy. Adding any heat to a coop will have to be a decision you make based on your weather patterns. In my area, even if we get extreme cold for our region, I do not add heat to the coop. When I open the coop in the morning, the birds are active and it is warm in there just from their combined body heat.

Dealing with heat is another matter, for us. It gets extremely hot and humid here as a rule in the summer months. We usually buy a couple of box fans from a large retailer in the spring. One gets hung up above the doorway to the coop, pointed towards the back window for cross ventilation. This fan runs from June through September with out a break, unless we get an unusual cool spell. This is why I buy two fans. Almost every year, one fan will die an early death from the use and dust and stop working. Yes, this could be a fire hazard, but we check it regularly for overheating and dust it to keep it as clean as possible. When the first fan dies, we have a back up to hang and get us through the rest of the warm weather.

Other ways to keep your chickens cool include providing plenty of fresh cool water, offering herbs frozen in ice cubes, chilled fruit such as watermelon, and making sure there is shade.

Photo Credit Leigh Schilling Edwards

Chicken Behavior and Management

Pecking order

Help combat this by giving the chickens plenty of room to get away from higher ranking chickens.

Sometimes, removing or placing the biggest bully into a chicken "time out" for a few days is enough to restructure the pecking order. When the bully is reintroduced to the flock it will be at a lower level in the newly established pecking order and this alone may break the habit.

Another way to combat boredom is to spread out some straw or hay and throw some scratch on time of the it. The chickens will be kept busy looking for the scatch.

Cannibalism- Prevent crowding and boredom and over heating.

Cover any red, bloody or pecked areas with BlueKote to prevent more pecking. Chickens are attracted to red and will peck at the sore, bloody area out of curiosity, leading to a more serious wound.

Dust Bath- chickens bathe by lying in a sandy, or dusty area and proceed to clean themselves in an interesting way. Don't be alarmed if your chicken looks distressed and is lying on its side and flapping around. This is dust bathing. It can be alarming the first time you see it. You can also use Diatomaceous Earth as a dust bath medium. Diatomaceous Earth DE powder is a natural substance which also has some insect killing properties in it. DE powder also is a drying agent and will help you keep the coop smelling fresh.

Recipe for Chicken Dust Bath

Wood ash

DE powder

Very dry soil

Mix all ingredients together and put in a shallow plastic baby pool, landscaping prefab pond, shallow cardboard box or a shallow hole.

Provide a dust bath and on a warm sunny day you may find your chickens enjoying a bath!

What to do if you get a Rooster?

No one can give you a one hundred percent guarantee that all of your hatchlings will be pullets. Even the best hatcheries can only be right 80 to 90 percent of the time. So, know that you have the chance of ending up with a rooster. Maybe you can keep him. Maybe you will have a docile one that will protect your hens, fertilize the eggs in case you want to hatch out chicks on your own, or maybe you just enjoy the antics and colorful feathers of a rooster. Great! But what if you can't. Going into this chicken raising arena, it is good to have a plan B in place, for roosters, hens that don't get along, or any possible events in the future. There are a few possibilities of how to deal with an unwanted rooster. Pin a note up at your local feed store. Some people are looking for roosters to fertilize their hens eggs. Use him to feed your family, is an often overlooked alternative in today's society, but was what was done routinely in history. So, your basic choices are keep him, find him a home or freezer camp.

Now, let me tell you a couple of unpopular ways to handle the situation. 1. Don't take him back to the store where you bought the hatchlings. They probably told you that there was no guarantee that you would have hens. Call the store and explain your predicament. They may know of someone looking for a rooster. 2. Don't take your rooster and drop it off at a local farm. First, biosecurity is an important factor to consider.

Your rooster may bring in a disease that is not present on that farm. And two, it's just not the good thing to do. Be responsible with your animal until you find another workable situation.

Sick Chickens

Always separate sick or weakened chickens from the flock. This is good practice for any flock or animal management. When separating, make sure they are safe from predators, as they would be if in the main coop. Have food and water available at all times. Make sure the sick room is not in direct sunlight or drafts, but is well ventilated.

It is true that chickens do not do well when alone. However, it is also true that illness can spread quickly. When deciding whether to give the weakened chick a buddy or not, realize the risks involved. This is not a decision I can make for you, but needs to be made on a case by case basis. I have had success in both ways of handling the sick or weakened chicken issue.

A Few Cautions

Wash your hands before and after handling any chicks or chickens.

Do not return any sick or dead chicks to the retail location where you bought them. If necessary, call the store and report the loss or illness and what you are seeing. Most retailers have a no refund policy because chicks are fragile beings. After they leave the store, the store personnel have no control over how they were kept or handled, which is why stores are not allowed to accept returns once the birds leave the store. This is regulated by the Department of Agriculture in most cases. If you notice signs of genuine illness, let the store know. They may need to call the hatchery to report a problem.

Don't Overreact Unfortunately, baby chicks are fragile. In nature, even with the best broody hen, not all chicks will survive. Keeping the brooder temperature set correctly and supplying fresh food and clean water will go a long way towards a successful chick rearing experience.

It is hard to find a vet that can or will treat chickens and other poultry. Learn all you can about common chicken ailments and be ready to treat minor issues yourself.

Worming

Many new chicken owners ask about worming chickens. Our recommendation is to make sure you know what you are treating before you give medications to your chickens. You can take a fecal sample to a vet office for testing. There are ways to combat intestinal worms before they occur by using some natural products on a daily or weekly basis. Pumpkin seeds, apple cider vinegar, garlic and DE powder are known to have properties that keep the chicken's digestive track functioning well.

Flying out of the Coop

Depending on your set up, you may find your chickens flying out of the fenced in yard. It is possible and fairly easy to trim the flight feathers on the chickens to keep them flying at a lower level.

Hold the chicken securely against your body to control one wing. Gently extend the other wing and locate the flight feathers

Using sharp scissors cut the flight feathers off evenly, taking off about 2 inches of growth. Repeat after each molt if necessary.

Photo Credit Leigh Schilling Edwards

Scaley Mites on Legs- Coat the chicken's legs with mineral oil. It smothers the mites and the condition clears up quickly

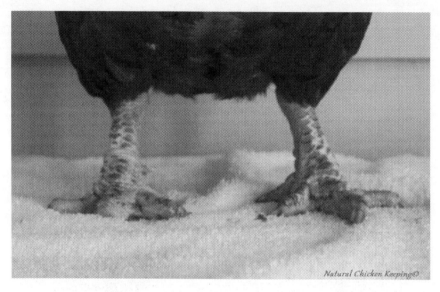

Photo Credit Leigh Schilling Edwards

Bumble Foot

If you notice one of your chickens holding one leg off the ground, or hopping instead of normal chicken walking take a look at the bottom of the feet. If you see a large bulge on the foot or toe, you may have a case of bumble foot. Bumble foot is a staphylococcus infection in the soft tissue. We have had a few cases of it here both in the chickens and the ducks but it is possible to successfully treat it yourself, and have no lasting side effects. Wear disposable examination gloves, so you don't transmit the bacteria to yourself or other members of the flock.

My preference is to treat with Vetrycin spray, an antibacterial spray, sold in many farm and pet supply shops. You may be able to avoid cutting into the foot if you start treatment early enough. Spray the area and wrap the foot in clean gauze and vet wrap. I then secure the wrapping job with a short piece of electric tape, which is the best waterproof tape I have found.

If the abscess does not start to heal while using this method you may need to carefully use a scalpel to open the abscess and release the pressure and the "corn" that is usually formed inside. There may be a great deal of puss or just a little and this is of course not for the faint of heart. ***If you are not comfortable with this procedure, please seek a veterinarian's assistance***.

Keep the affected foot bandaged until it is completely healed and the chicken is no longer limping. Keep in mind that my advice is only from my own experiences and I am not a veterinarian and do not practice medicine.

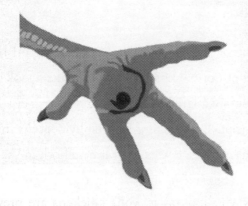

Predators

No matter how you look at it, your chickens are prey. Everything from raccoons, foxes, hawks, feral cats, and neighborhood dogs will be looking for a free meal. A large snake will eat a baby chick. The full grown hens will think the snake is a large worm and try to eat it. But the snake will be an egg thief. It is up to you to provide a safe habitat for your chickens. To free range your flock or not is a decision that you should make only after assessing the risks. Do you plan to free range only when you are keeping watch? You can be sure that if you have foxes in your area, they are keeping watch on your flock too. They are not only hunting in the evening. Raccoons will be an evening problem in all areas. When the young raccoons start growing up and hunting for their own food, they are a big problem for us.

CHICKENS FROM SCRATCH

Each area of the world has its own specific predators that you need to be aware of when raising small livestock. In our area, the east coast of the United States, I do not have to worry about bears, bob cats, and wolves. But raccoons, foxes and hawks can certainly do a lot of damage to a backyard or small farm flock of hens. Being aware of what you need to prepare against will go a long way toward successful chicken keeping. Your local extension service is a great resource for information on the natural predators in your area.

Photo Credit Leigh Schilling Edwards

First Aid Supplies

Any home, including and especially homesteads and farms should have basic first aid supplies on hand. The following is my recommended list of what to keep on hand for emergencies. We often use these for ourselves when a cut or sting occurs while tending to chores.

Saline Solution
Hydrogen Peroxide
Electrolytes powder
Gauze pads
Tweezers
Iodine/Betadine solution
Syringe
Corn starch or Wonder Dust
Neosporin
Cotton Swabs
Blue Kote
Paper towels, old towels, rags, old t-shirt material
Electric tape
Vaseline or Waxelene (for lubricant or protective coating)
Vet wrap
Vetrycin antibacterial spray for wound care

Tetrymycin ointment for eye injuries. (usually, must obtain through a vet)

A large towel to wrap an injured animal in. This will save you many bites and scratches when tending an injured animal

I hope this book has been helpful in starting your journey into raising chickens. I hope your chickens bring you as much joy as mine have brought into my life. Relax and enjoy their antics and personalities! And of course enjoy those farm fresh eggs! If you are looking for more information on chickens, ducks, rabbits, sheep, goats and other livestock, I would be honored if you would visit my website,

http://timbercreekfarmer.com

And here are some other very reputable resources for chicken information

www.fresheggsdaily.com
www.naturalchickenkeeping.com
http://www.happy-days-farm.com/
http://bornagainfarmgirl.blogspot.com/
www.homsteadbloggersnetwork.com
www.backyardpoultrymag.com
www.betterhensandgardens.com
www.fromscratchmag.com

Storeys Guide to Raising Chickens (ISBN-13: 978-1603424691)

Acknowledgements

There are many people who cheered me on as I took my first step into writing a book. This book may not be the longest book ever written on chicken care, in fact it may be one of the shortest. It took me a few years to bring to completion, and I rewrote much of it many times. Learning on the farm is a journey and not a destination. Thank you to three people in particular, for their encouragement, and for trying to keep me focused and on track, not and easy task. Thank you Hannah, Kat and Cheryl. I am continually learning and being amazed at how much my animals teach me every day. I thank you for reading my words on raising chickens, as naturally as possible.

A big thank you to my editing team who reviewed and edited this book.

Susan Brown, my dear friend for life and editor extraordinaire. I never knew I used so many commas in all the wrong places! The things we have been through over the years would require an entire new book, so a mere thank you will have to be enough.

Lisa Steele from www.fresheggsdaily.com - Thanks for reading my manuscript and evaluating the content. You started me on this trip of blogging a few years ago, and its been quite a ride! Thank you for your friendship and mentoring.

Angela England, www.AngEngland.com, for being a great teacher and mentor on the whole writing and publishing process.

Chris Daizel from www.joybileefarm.com - Thank you for reading my work, early on and making some valuable suggestions on the content. You share you experiences and knowledge so willingly and it is much appreciated.

My family was a big source of strength and encouragement as I dove into this project and determined to make it a reality. Gary, Chris, Ali, Michelle, Sean, Reagan, Nick, Samantha, TJ, my mom and my sister. Thank you for believing in me and helping me follow my dream.

And last but not least, the friends I have made through my blog and website, who have encouraged me to stretch, grow and learn new things. I used to think I was pretty techy, but you all have taught me so much more about the world of blogging and writing and publishing my work. Thank you.

Chicken Care Notes

1. _____
2. _____
3. _____
4. _____
5. _____
6. _____
7. _____
8. _____
9. _____
10. _____
11. _____
12. _____
13. _____
14. _____

15. _____

16. _____

17. _____

18. _____

19. _____

20. _____